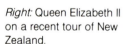 A family in the news

You cannot get away from the royal family in Britain. Switch on the television and they may well be on the news. There may be a film of the whole royal family attending a church service, or of a royal visit abroad. You may be familiar with pictures of the queen watching native dancers in costume. Or she may have been inspecting well-drilled soldiers. You will have seen such images many times. Of course, the queen is used to seeing such displays. She has seen thousands of them during her reign, it is all part of her job!

But why is all this on television? It is because the royal family makes news. Open a newspaper. How many articles deal with 'the royals'? Listen to the radio – there they are again!

Monarchs outside Britain

The British monarchy is a lonely one. There are few kings and queens left in the rest of Europe. Once, all Europe was ruled by powerful monarchs. Gradually, other countries have rejected their monarchs. For instance, members of the royal families of Greece and Russia have survived – but they are no longer crowned monarchs. These European royal families were often related to each other. British princesses were married off to foreign rulers. Now very few of the British queen's relatives are lucky enough to have a throne.

How did the British keep their throne when so many European 'royals' lost theirs? To answer this, we must look far into the past, to the time when Europe was ruled by kings.

The rule of kings

Once, British kings, and French and Spanish kings too, had real power. They punished their enemies and rewarded trusted followers. They made laws and led armies. Look at the cartoons on the right of the Tudor king, Henry VIII (1509–47) and the Stuart king, James I (1603–25). Read what each had to say about monarchy.

The Tudor and Stuart kings had no doubt who was boss in Britain. They were 'God's lieutenants' – his second in command. Anyone who disobeyed them was disobeying God. They could claim these great powers because there was no written 'constitution' (a sort of book of rules saying precisely who is in charge, and defining what a ruler can and cannot do). Many countries do have constitutions: but no such thing existed in Great Britain then.

Right: Queen Elizabeth II on a recent tour of New Zealand.

4

2·95

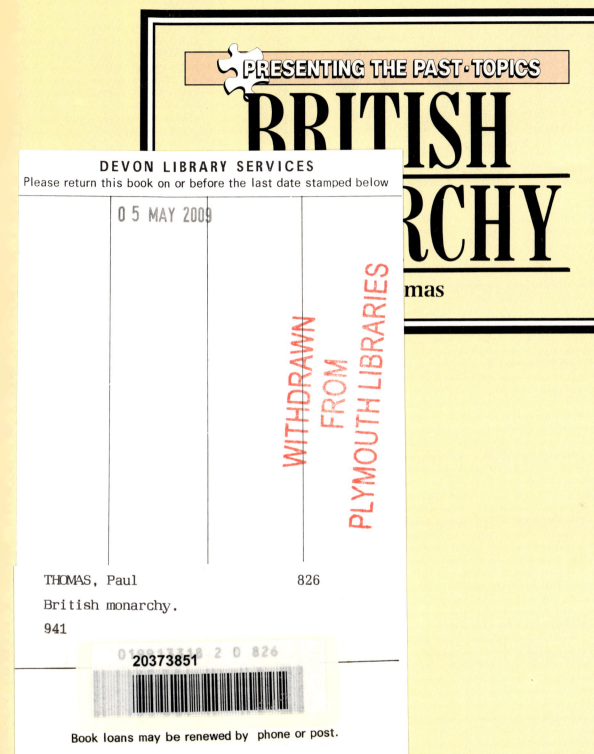

PRESENTING THE PAST · TOPICS

BRITISH MONARCHY

...mas

Oxford University Press 1989

JAMES I (VI OF SCOTLAND) 1603 – 25

CHARLES I 1625-49

CHARLES II 1660-85

Contents

ANNE 1702-14

GEORGE IV 1820-30

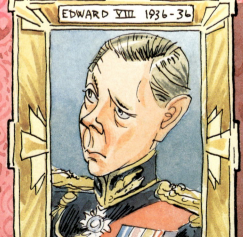

EDWARD VIII 1936-36

"(God) has set up princes as representatives of his own image to ordinary men, to be reputed as the highest and most superior of all creatures..... By me (God says) Kings reign....whoever disobeys the authority of a King disobeys the law of God."

"The monarchy is the most important thing on earth: for Kings are not only God's lieutenants on earth, and sit upon God's throne; but even by God himself they are called Gods"

IRELAND

Limits to the king's power

Magna Charta

Although there was no constitution, some rules had been drawn up long before. In 1215, the knights and nobles of England had quarrelled with King John (1204–16). He was said to be cowardly and dishonest. His knights did not trust him, and they ganged up on him and made him sign a new set of rules. This was called the Great Charter or, in Latin, *Magna Charta*. It limited John's power, and gave the knights a greater share in running the kingdom.

The *Magna Charta* set some limits to the power of the king. Soon the barons and gentlemen of England found another way to challenge their rulers: They used Parliament. English kings first called Parliament for help and advice, and also for permission to collect extra money when it was needed.

Parliament was a gathering of the richest and most important men in the kingdom. One group sat in the House of Lords, so-called because it contained the great lords and bishops of the kingdom, and members of the royal family. Because it was close to the king it was at first more important than the other group – the House of Commons. The House of Commons was not really 'common' at all. In fact there were usually *more* knights, gentlemen and lawyers in it than commoners.

Increasingly, as the business of ruling became more complicated, kings made the two Houses pass many laws. As more laws were passed, the king and his subjects were given more rules, and the lawyers and gentlemen in the House of Commons who helped pass them became more important. Then, King Henry VIII used Parliament to back him up in his quarrel with the Catholic Pope in Rome. With Parliament's help between 1529 and 1536, Henry took England out of the Catholic Church and set it on the road to becoming a Protestant country. In return, Parliament expected the king to protect the new religion. Henry VIII had added a new title to his name. He was called the 'Defender of the Faith.' In future all English rulers were expected to live up to this title, and resist the Roman Catholics, both inside England and abroad. □

Above: Three kings who had strong ideas about kingship. From the left: king Henry VIII (1509–1547), king John (1204–1216) and king James I (1603–1625).

1 Get a selection of newspapers, such as *The Daily Mirror, The Daily Mail, The Sun,* and *The Star.* How many stories deal with the royal family? What are the stories about? Do you think they're interesting? Say why or why not.

2 Now watch the news on television. Again, how many 'royal' stories are there? Are the stories sadder or happier than the rest of the news? If they are happier, do you think there's a special reason for showing them?

2 Parliament vs. king

Parliament and king quarrelled in the seventeenth century. In 1621, Parliament told James I:

> that the arduous and urgent affairs concerning the king, state and defence of the realm, and the maintenance and making of laws, and redress of complaints are proper subjects for counsel and debate in Parliament.

The members of the House of Commons claimed a right to advise and check up on the king about all sorts of important matters. Charles I himself admitted to being part of a team. In 1640 he said:

> In this Kingdom the laws are jointly made by a king, by a House of Lords, and by a House of Commons chosen by the people.

But both sides disagreed about what share of power each part of the team should have. Parliament accused the king of breaking his own laws, including Magna Charta. In 1642 the king's supporters, known as the 'cavaliers', fought the English civil war against Parliament's soldiers, the 'roundheads.'

Above: This painting by the Flemish painter, van Dyck, shows the royal family in 1632. Charles I (1625–1649) is seen with his wife, Henrietta Maria, and two of their children.

England becomes a republic

On trial

Charles' cavaliers lost. Parliament put him on trial and executed him. In 1649, the monarchy was abolished by a document which stated:

'Charles Stuart has been, and is hereby declared, put to death by authority derived from Parliament, for many treasons, murders, and other terrible offences … It has been found by experience that the office of king … is unnecessary, burdensome and dangerous to the liberty, safety and public interest of the people.'

Of course, Charles had not actually murdered anybody, but he was blamed for the deaths during the English civil war. Now Parliament had announced that England did not need a monarchy. So England became a 'republic'.

A republic is a state without a king. In such a state all the people see themselves as rulers, or, more often, they elect representatives to do the ruling for them. There is a *public* government, not a government belonging to a private owner – a royal owner. This was rather a new idea back in 1649, and it made England rather unusual. Countries were not used to doing without a king. When peasants, workers, and soldiers tried to make the republic represent them, the richer classes of people hurriedly put their trust in a new ruler. This was Oliver Cromwell (lived 1599–1658). He was a general who tried to rule with the help of Parliament, and was even offered the crown himself.

When Cromwell died in 1658 there was chaos. Several generals tried to take power. Religious maniacs plotted and rebelled. Wild revolutionaries preached the need for a democratic republic that would help the poor and attack the rich. The rich, and the middling sort of people took fright. A king would be better than such wild and dangerous ideas – even a Stuart king! And so Charles II, the dead king's son, was invited to take over.

More trouble

Charles II (ruled 1660–85) needed to treat Parliament well. If not he might be sent away again. A wily man, he usually got his own way and he kept his throne till the day he died a natural death. His brother James II (ruled 1685–88) was less clever and was driven out of England in a very short time indeed! James was a Roman Catholic and made no secret of the fact. He gave Catholics the best jobs in the army and government. Soon the English became afraid that he was going to make England a Catholic country again. In 1688, seven important politicians invited a new king to come to England. He was William, the prince of Orange. He was Dutch, but was married to Mary, James II's daughter. More important, William III (ruled 1689–1702) was a Protestant.

'The Great Deliverer' and 'English' Anne

The English called William 'the Great Deliverer' but he only 'delivered' England from the Catholics because he needed help against Louis XIV of France. He swiftly persuaded the English Parliament to vote to join the 'Nine Years War' (1689–97) against the French. William then spent his last years preparing for yet another war – the War of the Spanish Succession (1702–13).

William III was succeeded by another of James II's daughters, Queen Anne (ruled 1702–14). Anne firmly pointed out to Parliament that she was 'entirely English'. Her Englishness made her very popular with the public who had never really trusted William the Dutchman.

A German prince for Britain

In 1701, Parliament realized that the unlucky Anne was not likely to produce a healthy child, despite the fact that she had been pregnant 18 times. She would be the last monarch of the Stuart family. Parliament dare not give the throne to Anne's brother James for he had been brought up as a Catholic. But the royal family had distant relatives who were electors, or rulers, of the small state of Hanover (in modern Germany). They, at least, were Protestants. Parliament was careful to point out that:

Left: William III (1689–1702) and Mary. William's mission in life was to save the Netherlands from the attacks of the French. During his reign he had plenty of help from England to fight his enemies.

66 the laws of England are the birthright of the English people. All the kings and queens, who shall ascend the throne of this realm, ought to administer the government, according to these laws. 99

In a law called the Act of Settlement (1701), Parliament offered the throne of England to the German princes of Hanover:

66 For a further provision of the succession of the crown in the Protestant line. 99

Things had changed a great deal since the days of Henry VIII. English kings could no longer think of themselves as 'God's lieutenants'. They were kings because Parliament wanted them to do a job. They were needed to keep England Protestant at all costs. Kings were there to protect England from the chaos and wild politics that had frightened respectable people during the years of the republic.

The monarchy's responsibilities had, too, been extended to include the full government of Scotland. The crowns of England and Scotland had been united in 1603, under James I, who was already King James VI of Scotland before he acquired the English throne. When it was clear that the Scottish Stuarts would no longer rule after Anne died, it was decided to bring Scottish government firmly under English control. In the Act of Union (1707), Scotland became part of Great Britain. □

Above: Queen Anne (1702–1714). While queen Anne was dying, her Tory ministers fought over who would succeed her.

1 William of Orange was Dutch, he knew that the English Parliament quarrelled with the king of England. He also knew that in 1649 they'd executed an English king. What doubts might William have had about accepting the English invitation to become king in 1688?

Unhappy families

Above: George I (1714–1727).

Below: George II (1727–1760).

In 1714, Elector George of Hanover became King George I of Great Britain of England, Wales and Scotland. With him, the Whig party came to power. These were the supporters of the 1688 revolution and of the power of Parliament. The king had been invited over on their terms. The new royal family, the Hanoverians, were not happy. Years before, George I had quarrelled with his wife, Sophia Dorothy. He divorced her, locked her up in a castle for the rest of her life, and, it was rumoured, murdered her boyfriend.

The future George II, hated his father. The feeling was mutual. In 1717, father and son fell out publicly. The prince and his wife were banished from court. After that there were two rival courts. The king's friends and ministers met at the *official* court at St James' Palace in London. The younger generation, and the opponents of the government, met at Leicester House in London with the prince and princess. There they planned for the day when the prince would become king.

The rules of the game

The Leicester House politicians called themselves Whigs. The king's government was run by Whigs. In fact only one party had any real chance of power. The Tories had disgraced themselves by supporting the claims of the Catholic Stuarts. Ambitious Tories gave up and joined the Whigs. Each group of Whigs hoped to join the government. This would give them power and they could reward their friends with jobs and influence. Politics was a game of *ins* and *outs*. If you were *in*, you enjoyed the glories and opportunities of governing Great Britain. If you were *out* you went to Leicester House. You then hoped to make such a nuisance of yourself that the government would give in and ask you to join. Although you needed supporters in the House of Commons to force your way into the government, there was one other vital ingredient: this was the support of the king. He, and he alone, could pick or dismiss ministers.

The first prime minister

One man above all others, played this game and won. He was Sir Robert Walpole, and he is generally thought of as the first real prime minister of England. His power irritated his rivals. With him at the top, other ambitious Whigs had no chance. In 1741, one member of parliament complained

'According to our constitution, we can have no sole and prime minister: we ought always to have several officers of state ... But it is publicly known that Mr Walpole has monopolized all the favours of the crown.'

The queen and the courtier

In 1727, the old king died. In Leicester House the prince of Wales and Walpole's enemies rejoiced. It seemed their chance had come. The new king, George II, tried to sack Walpole and put a friend, Spencer Compton, in his place. But, as a courtier, Lord Hervey, said:

66 As soon as ever the prince became king, the whole world began to find out that the queen's will was the sole spring on which every movement in the court turned. It is an undoubted fact that she

chose Walpole. By her influence the king, though he disliked him ... employed him. 🗩🗩

George II's brilliant and beautiful wife, Queen Caroline of Anspach, ruled the court and the king. The cunning Walpole used his friendship with her to keep his job. Until her death in 1737, he was safe. Even then, George II kept on the minister who had by then, won his trust.

The Hanoverians settle in

However, George II was hardworking and conscientious. He insisted on reading and signing all important paperwork. He was also the last soldier-king of Britain. In 1744, he led his army on the battlefield of Dettingen against the French. He was also lucky. Walpole gave his king 20 years of peacetime prosperity. Then, when times changed and the English called for war against the traditional enemies (France and Spain), a great wartime leader emerged to serve him. This was William Pitt the Elder who organized the greatest victories the English had enjoyed for centuries in the *Seven Years' War* (1756–63). So when George II died in 1760, the author, Horace Walpole (Robert Walpole's son) felt that he died:

66 Full of years and glory, without a pang and without a defeat. He left his family firmly established on a long-disputed throne. 🗩🗩

But there *had* been serious problems. The throne had been disputed by the 'Jacobites' in rebellions in 1715 and 1745. Often the English suspected their German kings of 'selling out' to their foreign interests in Hanover. However, George II's reign was generally seen as a time of great success. The English were proud of their victories, proud of their navy, and proudest of all of their freedom. Some of the most vivid pictures of freedom and success were created by the artist William Hogarth (1697–1764). But this freedom was soon to seem under threat. ☐

Left: Queen Caroline of Anspach, wife of George II. This clever and powerful woman was the key to prime minister Robert Walpole's success during her husband's reign.

Below: William Hogarth's painting was originally called 'O the Roast-Beef of Old England'. The freedom of the beef-eating English is contrasted with the cowering French and sinister priests in Calais. The sad looking Scots soldier was probably a recently defeated Jacobite. The Jacobites tried to win back the throne of England for the Stuart family.

1 A German king has arrived on the throne. Imagine you are a patriotic English citizen. Write a short speech explaining why you would prefer an English king or queen.

2 We rarely hear of quarrels in the present day royal family. Perhaps they don't dislike each other as much as the Hanoverians did. Some reasons have been suggested for the Hanoverians quarrels. Can you think of any others?

3 Why did Hogarth make a fuss about roast beef (see above)? Do we still eat it as an English dish? If not, why not?

4 The Jacobites probably had a rather exciting life as they sneaked back and forth between England, France, and Scotland. Imagine you are a Jacobite. Suggest why you would prefer a Stuart to a Hanoverian king.

4 'Tyrant' George

In 1760, George I's grandson, George III, became king. He meant well, but his methods of ruling soon became controversial, as these remarks show:

66 The power of the Crown has grown up anew with much more strength and far less odium, under the name of influence.　(Edmund Burke *Thoughts on the Causes of the Present Discontents*, 1769)

The Queen Mother is secretly acknowledged the governess or mistress general of both Lords and Commons.
　(*The Constitutional Guardian*, 1770)

The influence of the Crown has increased, is increasing and ought to be diminished.　(John Dunning, 1781)

At your accession to the throne the whole system of government was altered: not from wisdom or deliberation, but because it had been adopted by your predecessor. A little personal motive of pique and resentment was sufficient to remove the ablest servants of the crown. 99　(*Junius*, 1769)

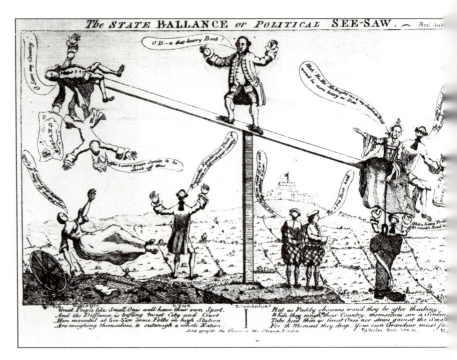

Above: The references to 'Boot' in this cartoon are to the earl of Bute.

Below: George III and his family.

Clearly something went terribly wrong for the new king. Edmund Burke, a famous politician in the new reign, seemed to see a new royal power emerging. His friend, the lawyer John Dunning, saw it too and called it *influence*.

George's mother was accused of being a power behind the throne. So, too, was George's friend and tutor, Lord Bute. Junius, an anonymous newspaper author, went to the root of the problem. The old hatred from Leicester House (see page 8) came back in 1760.

George III had been brought up by his mother and Bute to hate his grandfather's ministers. He had been taught to see the great Whig politicians as corrupt and self-interested. Quickly he got rid of the wartime ministers, William Pitt and his Whig friends. The king announced that he 'gloried in the name of Britain.' He contrasted his own entirely British background with the German sympathies of George II.

The reign started badly when the king replaced the old ministers with his friend, John Stuart, the earl of Bute, as prime minister. Bute's Scottish name of Stuart upset people who vividly remembered the Scottish Jacobite rebellion of 1745. Worse, Bute was totally inexperienced. How could he become prime minister when the *real* professionals like Pitt were ready and waiting to take over?

George III had to send for one of the professionals. Reluctantly, he chose George Grenville. Some called Grenville a pompous windbag, but he was an able politician.

An unforgiving master

Grenville soon discovered the cost of angering this young king. Although a clever man, Grenville was a dreadful bore. Believing Bute was still influencing the king, he nagged George and lectured him endlessly. The king complained:

66 When he has wearied me for two hours he looks at his watch to see if he may not tire me for an hour more. 99

By 1765, George III had had enough. He sacked Grenville. Naturally Grenville blamed Bute's 'secret influence'.

The king was an unforgiving master and there were severe penalties to pay for offending him. When the flamboyant and immoral John Wilkes angered him in 1763, the king sought revenge for many years. He had Wilkes outlawed, tried, imprisoned, and banned from Parliament. Charles James Fox insulted the king over the Royal Marriage Act (1772), and abused him in many House of Commons speeches. He also introduced George's sons to the delights of drinking and gambling, and yet was surprised to be excluded from George's government from 1785 to 1805.

The king's government on the ropes

Wilkes became a public hero. For years he led the mob against the government. Few had a good word to say for George and his ministers. A new prime minister, the duke of Grafton, actually fled from London to escape the rioting of Wilkes' followers in 1769. Meanwhile, the American colonists defied the government (see page 12). They too rioted and jeered at authority. In America and England, Wilkes was showered with presents and a new voice joined in. This was 'Junius'. He hid his identity while,

for three years, he filled the papers with his poisonous and sarcastic criticisms of the government. Furious ministers took journalists, booksellers, and printers before the courts and the Houses of Parliament. At stake was the right to print criticism of the government, and to publish and discuss the business of Parliament. Although Wilkes' wild abuse in the *North Briton* newspaper had him arrested, other papers took up his theme. Although several printers were condemned for publishing parliamentary debates, the principle was won and the debates continued to appear. The basic freedom of the English press had been achieved. And Junius? We still don't know for sure who he was. □

John Wilkes was an ambitious journalist. He claimed to fight for freedom of the press and the liberties of all Englishmen. His continual attacks on George III and the government gained him lots of support with the general public. But the king did not like Wilkes, nor his wild lifestyle, and had him arrested more than once.

1 Bute and the queen mother were much attacked in the newspapers. Write a short letter to an imaginary newspapers:
a) saying everything wrong about George III and his supporters; b) Defending the king and attacking Wilkes.

2 Wilkes was a popular hero, an expert swordsman, and a successful writer – he was as famous as perhaps a pop star is today. Think of the way the papers write about pop stars. Now write a description of Wilkes' adventures.

3 Grenville and others believed Bute had a secret influence after he had retired. Suggest some ways in which Bute might have been able to 'influence' the king.

5 The world turned upside down

When general Burgoyne surrendered his English army to the victorious American rebels at Saratoga in 1778, the band played the tune 'the world turned upside down'. It was indeed a topsy-turvy world. And in it, the English monarchy was to survive by the skin of its teeth . . .

The Age of Revolution begins

The war of American Independence lasted from 1775 to 1783. The Americans challenged the British in their Declaration of Independence (1776). This put the blame for the war squarely onto George III:

66 The history of the present king is a history of repeated injuries and interference . . . he has ravaged our coasts, burnt out towns . . . his character is thus marked by every act which may define a tyrant. He is unfit to be the ruler of a free people. 99

This savage attack on George is rather like the condemnation of Charles I (page 6). The age of revolution had started. It was soon to become an age of king-killers.

Above: George III feels the threats of the war of American Independence and the French Revolution.

Rebellion

The French helped the Americans in their war against the English. Many Frenchmen learned from the American rebels.

In 1789, the French, too, had a revolution. In 1793, they executed their king, Louis XVI. What is more, they called out to the other peoples of Europe. They called for world revolution – for the end of kings *everywhere*!

A mad king

At this time of crisis, with the English monarchy itself under threat, the king of England went mad. One observer commented, as the king slid into madness in the autumn of 1788,

66 During the whole music he talked continually, making frequent and sudden changes from one subject to another . . . his great hurry of spirits and his wild talkativeness . . . gave great uneasiness to the queen. 99

The king's illness started a political crisis. He was too ill to rule. Surely his son, George, the prince of Wales, should take over?

But all his sons were wild, extravagant and too fond of gambling and the ladies. Their antics made the English monarchy a laughing

Right: Louis XVI was beheaded in 1793. So was his queen, Marie Antoinette. Thousands of killings followed their deaths in what was called the Reign of Terror (1794–5). These killings dismayed many Englishmen, and soon England was at war with France.

stock. The nation had to pay off the princes' large debts. At a time of war and revolution, the poor soon came to hate such irresponsible extravagance.

Whig vs. Tory – again

Since about 1770, the king's friends and ministers had become known as Tories. The opposition naturally thought of themselves as Whigs (see page 8). The Hanoverian tradition of quarrels between father and son returned when prince George grew up. He became a Whig. If he was made regent, the Tory prime minister, William Pitt the younger, and his ministers would be sacked. In would come the Whigs, led by the prince's drinking pal, Charles James Fox. Soon the king was being visited by two sets of doctors. The Whig Dr Warren solemnly assured the world that the king was doomed – and that the regent should be sent for. Pitt brought in Dr Willis and son. They insisted, to Pitt's relief, that the king could be cured. The Willises were right. Within weeks the king was back to normal. The crisis was over. So were the hopes of the prince and the Whigs.

Father of jealousy

As George III grew old and ill, he became more cut off from his subjects. Many had been thrilled by the excitement and the aims of the French Revolution. Authors could now look at Pitt and the government and claim . . .

66 Pitt has neglected and by his wars and taxes oppressed the poor – praises a free constitution and tramples its laws underfoot. 99

These were the words of John Thelwall, an English revolutionary. As the English upper classes panicked, their fear of revolution made the government remove many of the English liberties that Hogarth and Wilkes had been so proud of. Freedom of speech, trial by jury, freedom from sudden arrest and imprisonment were swept away – in the name of the king. To many admirers of the French, George seemed a tyrant. The great poet and painter William Blake pictured George III as the:

66 Father of Jealousy . . . why art thou silent (he asked)
Why dost thou hide yourself in clouds
From every searching eye 99 . . . □

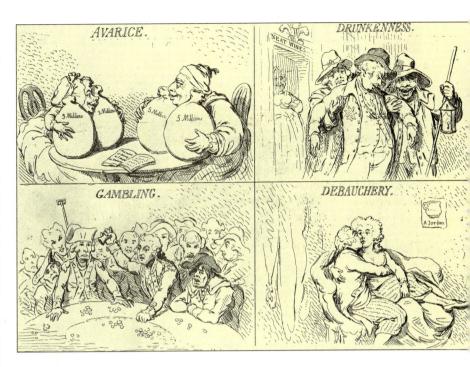

1 Look at the cartoon on page 12. Which three flags are shown? What do the colours of each flag represent?

2 Why did the English cheer the French Revolution at the start? Why did they turn against it later?

3 The methods of treating George III for madness were primitive. It must have seemed strange to the doctors, to treat a king. What worries might affect the doctors in treating a king? How do doctors deal with madness nowadays?

4 The royal dukes made themselves very unpopular. Write a short note suggesting what you think is the job of a royal prince. What should such public people not do? Why not?

This cartoon by James Gillray is a satire on George III and his family. 'Avarice' shows the king and queen, 'Drunkenness' the prince of Wales, 'Gambling' the duke of York and 'Debauchery' the duke of Clarence.

George III in his final illness. This picture showed the king's blindness and weakness so clearly that George IV tried to keep it hidden.

In 1811, George III went mad for the last time. He was never to recover. Deaf and blind, he grew his hair long, played his flute for hours on end – playing music he could not hear. And for hours he talked to courtiers, friends, and children – all of whom were long since dead.

The dandy of sixty

66 The Dandy of sixty, who bows with a
grace,
And has taste in wigs, collars,
waistcoats and lace
Who to tricksters, and fools, leaves the
State and its treasures,
And when Britain's in tears, sails about
his pleasures. 99 (*The Political House that
Jack Built*, 1819)

Meanwhile, the prince of Wales at last became prince regent, ruling in the place of his father. The prince was most unpopular in England, as the above verse shows. (A 'Dandy' was a fashion-conscious society figure, perhaps what we would today call a playboy). Prince George's extravagance was especially unpopular during and after the Napoleonic Wars, which finished with the Battle of Waterloo in 1815. Although it ended in a British victory, the war was followed by hard times. The poor of Britain were heavily taxed, unemployed, or simply starving. When they demonstrated in anger, the government sent spies to betray them, and soldiers to crush them.

Above: A peaceful protest demanding parliamentary reform was cut down by the cavalry at St Peter's Field, Manchester in 1819. To taunt the government with memories of Waterloo, the people swiftly renamed the event the Peterloo Massacre.

Below: The Brighton Pavilion, built on the instructions of George IV. The Regency period was a great time for architecture.

The regent had become a Tory. He had abandoned old friends like Fox, and promoted harsh Tory ministers to his government. He encouraged the government's grim policies against the British poor. When, in 1819, cavalry in Manchester cut down men, women and children during a peaceful protest (see above), George actually sent a letter of congratulation to the local authorities concerned. No wonder he was disliked.

No regrets

The Whigs, and the public, had a measure of revenge in 1820, when old George III died. This meant the regent became king, as George IV, and that his wife, princess Caroline of Brunswick, became queen. He had long hated her. She had left the country in 1814, but now returned to claim her rights, and wholly humiliated the new king. George never recovered from the shame he suffered over the Queen Caroline affair. Although he kept his throne until his death in 1830, the times were changing. The king's refusal to grant rights to the Catholics of Great Britain caused deep resentment, especially in Ireland (see opposite page). Although George eventually granted Catholic rights in 1828, he remained under great pressure to change the political system itself. This he would not do, and he refused point blank to

employ the Whigs in his government.

When he died no one seemed to care. He too had become a little mad, insisting that he, and not the duke of Wellington, was the victor of the Battle of Waterloo. A series of royal tours in the early 1820s seemed briefly to inspire a flicker of royal popularity. Official visits to Scotland and Ireland were greeted with great enthusiasm by the local people. A lavish coronation ceremony was popular with the Londoners. Perhaps such ceremonies and public appearances pointed the way ahead for a modern monarch? But George IV was too old and ill to keep it up. At his death, *The Times'* obituary was merciless:

> 66 Never was an individual less regretted by his fellow-creatures than this dead king. What eye has wept for him? If ever he had a friend, we protest that that friend's name never reached us. 99

The years 1811–30, when George IV was regent and king, mark a low point for the monarchy. Almost nobody liked George IV. Throughout these years revolution seemed just around the corner. A prime minister was assassinated in 1812, an attempt was made to blow up the entire cabinet in 1820. Yet, somehow the monarchy survived...

Reform or revolution

The new king was George's brother, William IV (1765–1837). He was already over 60 years old, and was not noted for his intelligence. But, after George IV, he was comparatively popular. This was just as well because, between 1830 and 1832, the British monarchy and political system faced its greatest crisis – the struggle for the 'Great Reform Act'. The British political system was badly out of date. In 1830, when the Whigs at last came to office, they were determined to bring change. Outside Parliament, the mob bayed for reform. They rioted, wrecked and burned. Revolution seemed very close. For two years, the king dithered and the House of Lords defied the mob and the Commons. Finally, in 1838, a Reform Act was passed. The system, and the king were safe. William had eventually given his support to the Whigs, the party of reform. He feared that otherwise:

> 66 The country would be thrown into chaos from Lands End to John O'Groats. 99

Above: The Irish rebellion of 1798 was put down with great cruelty. In the picture a pitch cap is being applied to an Irish Rebel. Both George III and IV believed that to improve the rights of Irish Catholics was going against their Coronation Oaths as Defenders of the Faith.

Without reform, change might have been violent and might have destroyed the monarchy. William, by helping the Whigs in 1832, probably saved the crown. He died in 1837. □

1 Do you think George IV was wrong to try to divorce his wife? Give reasons why you think it might have been: a) a mistake; and b) a good idea.

2 In what ways were George III and IV trying to defend the Faith in dealing with Catholics?

3 Imagine there was an English Revolution in 1832. What do you think would have happened?

Above: This sharp comment on George IV's habits also refers to the 'queen Caroline affair'. In spite of her sometimes odd behaviour, Caroline was more popular with the people than the king. There were celebrations all over the country when his attempts to divorce her failed.

7 The way forward

Above: Queen Victoria in her coronation robes

Right: Victoria married her cousin, the German prince Albert, in 1839. He was very active, interested in science and the welfare of the poor. Victoria relied heavily on his advice and support.

The rule of an ageing Dandy, and of his stupid brother, had brought the British monarchy to the brink of ruin. Political reform had come in 1832. Change was in the air. The future lay in the hands of a young girl. Queen Victoria was only 18 years old when she came to the throne in 1837. She was inexperienced, but very determined. When, as a child, she first learned that she would be queen when she grew up, she had stated firmly, 'I will be good'. But would she be good enough?

> ### The Constitutional Monarchy
> Victoria had inherited a thoroughly 'Constitutional' Monarchy. What did this mean? It meant that although there was no written constitution, the monarch was still bound by rules. These rules went back to *Magna Charta* (see page 5), and had gained enormously in force when Charles I was executed for breaking some of them (see page 6). The terms of Parliament's invitations to William III and George I (see page 7) had further limited the monarch's powers. So, too, had the years of George III's madness, and of the French wars.

Royal powers

The real governing of the country was now done by the prime minister and a cabinet of ministers. Where the monarch had previously been able to choose his or her own ministers, now he had to employ the leaders of whichever party won each general election. A monarch could however call and dismiss Parliament. He signed and inspected official documents.

Whig and Tory

As we have seen (see page 8), the terms Whig and Tory came back into use from about 1770. Generally, Whigs in opposition had got into the habit of calling all government politicians Tories. When Pitt and his followers had been in power for years they came to be called the Tories. They stood for the authority of Church of England and monarchy, and resisted reforms like Catholic Emancipation, or the Reform Act. In contrast, the Whigs saw themselves as a party of change and reform.

So, the young queen was faced with the duty of working with whichever of these two parties was voted in.

At first she would need all the help she could get, especially from experienced politicians. Two in particular helped enormously. These were her uncle, King Leopold of the Belgians, and the English politician, Lord Melbourne. Victoria had inherited a Whig government. Melbourne was the prime minister. His advice and encouragement were vital. Victoria considered him, 'the best-hearted, kindest and most feeling man in the world'. Victoria became an enthusiastic Whig. This gave the Whigs an unfair advantage over the Tories. In 1839, Victoria used her remaining powers to keep Lord Melbourne and the Whigs in power, and the Tories out.

The bedchamber crisis

The Whigs had been defeated in Parliament, and resigned. The Queen had to send for the leader of the Tories, Sir Robert Peel. Traditionally, a new prime minister and his party could expect the monarch to replace some household servants, giving the jobs of ladies of the bedchamber, and grooms, to important friends of the new government. It gave the new leader a chance to reward loyal supporters. Peel therefore expected Victoria to sack some of the Whig ladies, and replace them with Tory ladies. Victoria complained:

66 Peel has behaved very ill, and has insisted on my giving up my ladies, to which I replied that I would never consent, and I never saw a man so frightened – the Queen of England will not submit to such trickery. 99

An annoyed Peel resigned. The Whig queen kept her party in power for two more wretched years of government. Melbourne had the queen's support, but that was no longer enough to run a country. In 1841, a general election was well won by the Tories. Peel was back. Victoria was unhappy, but had learned her lesson. She wrote to a worried uncle Leopold, 'I beg you not to be alarmed . . . it is the fairest and most constitutional mode of proceeding.'

The queen's job

The queen's job changed in 1839 when she married the German, prince Albert. It became her task to have children to preserve the inheritance of her family. That inheritance was the throne of England.

Like George III, Victoria had a large family (see page 21). Its members all grew up and became adults while their mother was still on the throne. They therefore had to be kept busy. The royal family needed to be useful. This Victorian family developed a new and important role for itself, by creating many of the features of the modern day monarchy.

In 1867, the author Walter Bagehot wrote a book called *The English Constitution*. In it he examined the royal family's function. Why did the British have a Royal Family? Why did they pay for it? What use was it? He concluded:

66 The use of the Queen is incalculable. Constitutional Monarchy is strong because people understand it. Where a Republic has only difficult ideas, monarchy is easy. A family on the throne is an interesting idea also, it appeals to the level of normal life. No feeling could seem more childish than the enthusiasm of the English at the marriage of the prince of Wales. They treated as a great political event what was a small family matter. And we have come to regard the Crown as the head of our Morality. 99

Bagehot had seen what had happened. The royal family should act like an *ordinary* British family. Its births marriages and deaths should be like those of any other British family. The future of Royalty in Britain had been decided . . . ☐

Above: In 1851, the Great Exhibition was held in London at Hyde Park to display British goods and achievements.

Left: The English public were not too keen on Albert. He came from a part of Germany where parliaments were unusual and freedom of the press was unknown. He found the limits set on royal power very frustrating. During the Crimean War (1854–6) the newspapers demanded that the foreign prince be sent to the Tower of London. The Prime Minister at the time had to make a special statement in support of Albert to calm down public opinion.

1   Imagine it is late 1837. What do you think Queen Victoria's New Year resolutions might have been?

2   What do you think Lord Melbourne thought about the bedchamber crisis? What reservations would he have felt about its outcome?

3   What do you think was shown in the Great Exhibition? What do you think would be shown in a modern Great Exhibition?

8 The widow of Windsor

The happiest years of Victoria's life ended abruptly. In December 1861, her husband Albert died suddenly of fever. The queen declared herself:

66 an utterly broken-hearted and crushed widow of 42! My life as a happy one is ended. 99

Years of blank widowhood lay ahead of her. She was not to die till 1901. With Albert's death, the burdens of monarchy fell right back onto her shoulders. In 1852, she had commented that:

66 Albert grows daily fonder and fonder of politics and business, and is so wonderfully fit for both – I grow daily to dislike them both more and more. 99

Predictably, the grief-stricken queen performed her duties without enthusiasm. She withdrew from public life for years on end. This retirement led to yet another crisis for the monarchy. The public felt cheated. When would the 'widow of Windsor' return to her duties as queen of England?

Victoria in mourning

Victoria showed her love for Albert by having the Albert Memorial (see right) built in Hyde Park, London, and opposite that, the Albert Hall. Her grief caused problems. She lost interest in work. She preferred to remain behind closed doors in Buckingham Palace, or away from London, at Windsor, or in the Royal home at Balmoral in Scotland.

Another wicked prince?

Soon ugly rumours circulated that the queen was too friendly with one of Albert's old servants, a huge silent Scottish groom called John Brown. Meanwhile, her son the future Edward VII, the prince of Wales, seemed about to recreate the problems we saw caused by George III's sons (see page 13). It seemed that Edward, after a sheltered and strict upbringing, might, as an adult, be going the same way as the notorious royal dukes of the eighteenth century. He was seen too often in high society;

Above: Queen Victoria had the Albert Memorial built in London in honour of her late husband.

Right: The queen and her groom, John Brown, outside Osborne House on the Isle of Wight. Her familiarity with him led to public criticism. As a commoner he was seen as an unsuitable companion for a queen.

18

he gambled and attended horse races – he was involved in a divorce case. People began to talk of the prince as a public expense and nuisance. And, why should the public pay for an absent queen and a wicked prince?

The year 1871 was perhaps worst for Victoria. She was nervous and irritable. She felt nagged by her ministers. Edward was terribly ill, and nearly died of typhoid. Newspapers pried into royal finances and accused Victoria of 'hoarding' public money instead of spending it for its proper purposes.

Lectures for a queen

Victorian politics became more stable between 1868 and 1885, when two great leaders, Benjamin Disraeli and William Gladstone, dominated the scene. In 1859, various Whig politicians, reformers, and modern-minded Tories joined to found the Liberal party, which came to be headed by Gladstone. The remaining Tories went on, under Disraeli to form the Conservative party. Both parties were better organized, stricter in their loyalties, in short, more modern, than their Whig and Tory predecessors. And, both party leaders fought hard to get the queen back to work again.

Gladstone was honest, but tactless. 'He lectures me as if I was a public meeting', complained the queen (remember George Grenville and George III on page 9?). Gladstone told Victoria her duty. He bullied her. She detested this treatment and became obstinate. She threatened:

66 Unless her ministers support her – she cannot go on and must give up her heavy burden up to younger hands. 99

A BAD EXAMPLE.

Dr. Punch. "WHAT'S ALL THIS? YOU, THE TWO HEAD BOYS OF THE SCHOOL, THROWING MUD! YOU OUGHT TO BE ASHAMED OF YOURSELVES!"

Left: Victorian newspapers took great interest in the goings-on in the House of Commons. The debates in the Commons between Gladstone and Disraeli were of particular interest because the two men really did hate each other. The *Punch* cartoon is making fun of their hostility.

LONG LIVE OUR KING & QUEEN

Above: Edward, prince of Wales (later Edward VII) was queen Victoria's eldest son. He was very strictly brought up, probably because his parents feared the influence of the "wicked uncles" (what Victoria called George IV's sons). In fact the Prince did valuable work in keeping up public appearances when his mother was in mourning. He is shown here with his wife Alexandra.

'Help' for the monarchy

Two events helped the monarchy. One was Edward's illness, which won him immense public sympathy. The *Annual Register* of 1871 commented that 'the nation seemed to gather round the throne with a single heart and a single prayer.' The prince's recovery prompted a thanksgiving service. Then, after the service, a deranged youth aimed an empty pistol at the queen. A deeply shocked public again rallied to the monarchy.

A little flattery

Disraeli, who was prime minister in 1868 and from 1874–80, knew the way to Victoria's heart. 'Everyone likes flattery and when you come to Royalty, you should lay it on with a trowel', was his theory. The colourfully-dressed, dramatic, witty Disraeli charmed Victoria. He was more exciting, and more tactful than Gladstone. Like Lord Melbourne, he gave the queen much-needed guidance and confidence. The monarchy was back on the road again. Victoria, once a Whig, now identified with her friend Disraeli's party. She became a Conservative! □

1 a) For how long was Victoria a widow?
  b) How old was she when she died?

2 You are prime minister of England. It is your job to get Victoria back to work again after Albert's death. Explain to her what is wrong and what you want her to do: a) lecture her like Gladstone; b) be tactful like Disraeli.

9 Rule Britannia – empire years

Thanks to Disraeli's Royal Titles Act (1876), Victoria became the queen-empress, ruling over the exotic lands and teeming millions of India. The last 20 years of her reign witnessed the two great jubilee celebrations of 1887 and 1897 to mark the fiftieth and sixtieth years of her rule. In 1887 the Jubilee was a home-grown affair celebrated by the British, although several commonwealth prime ministers attended. In 1897, the salute to the queen also became a tremendous celebration of the British empire.

It had taken the English a while to learn to love their empire. Even Disraeli had once referred to the colonies as 'millstones round our necks.' The public were not at all sure about the queen's new title back in 1876. But in 1897 English people were proud to note that the British empire was bigger by far than the conquests of Julius Caesar and the Roman emperors. Over the years, too, the newspapers and popular novels had celebrated the exciting exploits of heroes like Gordon of Khartoum and Lord Kitchener. Such heroes probably had much the same appeal as pop stars do today.

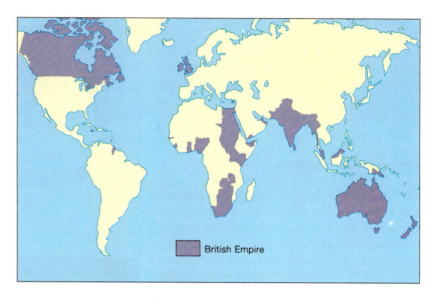

British Empire

Oh, if the queen were a man

Victoria was a most enthusiastic and patriotic queen. Her patriotism was simple and often very unreasonable. She unthinkingly hated the Russians. In 1878 the Music Halls of England rang with the 'Jingo' song:

> 66 We don't want to fight but by jingo if we do
> We've got the ships, we've got the men,
> We've got the money too. 99

Above: The British Empire at the time of Victoria's death in 1901.

Below: Queen Victoria is shown arriving at the steps of St Paul's Cathedral for the Diamond Jubilee Thanksgiving Service.

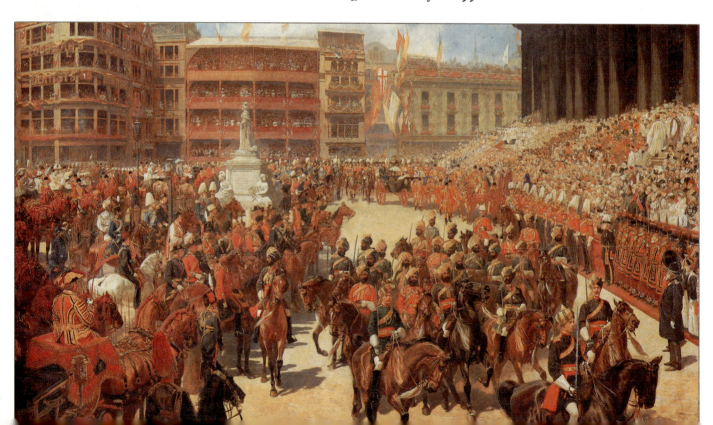

Britain and Russia seemed on the brink of war as they quarrelled about the Mediterranean and the future of Turkey. The queen was all for war. Victoria declared:

❝Oh if the Queen were a man, she would like to go and give those horrid Russians such a beating!❞

The Victoria Cross

Back in the Crimean War (1854–56), Queen Victoria had visited and praised her troops. 'I feel so much for them, and am so fond of my dear soldiers, and so proud of them', she declared. She awarded a special medal for *all* ranks – not merely for the officers who usually hogged all the glory – the Victoria Cross.

The Victoria Cross is still the highest decoration an English soldier can win.

End of an era

But the successful times were coming to an end. In the first years of Empire-building, British troops had it easy. Their guns and equipment were far superior to those of their opponents. Victories were cheaply won. When, in 1899, a long-standing row with the Dutch South Africans, the Boers, broke into open war, Victoria's soldiers were humiliated. In one 'Black Week', the British were three times defeated by a cunning, and well-armed enemy. Even Kipling, author of so many fiercely pro-empire poems, changed his tune:

❝Let us admit it fairly, as a business
    people should,
  We have had no end of a lesson;
  It will do us no end of good❞

It seemed a sad way for a long and successful reign to end. But in 1901 the old queen died. As one contemporary remarked, 'the vast majority of her subjects had never known a time when Queen Victoria had not been reigning over them'. It was the end of an era. □

Left: Paintings like this detail from *The Royal Horse Artillery under Fire* were very popular. They celebrated British victories.

1 Write an eight line poem about Queen Victoria. Be polite about her.

2 Look at the map of the old empire. Can you guess where Afghans, Zulus, Ashantis or Boers come from?

3 Pretend that you are Edward VII on Victoria's death. It has been a long wait. Write a letter to your subjects: a) summing up Victoria's achievements; b) explaining your own plans for the monarchy.

Above: This genealogical tree was produced to celebrate the fiftieth Jubilee. Try to identify Victoria and Albert's nine children, and their wives or husbands.

It was 1901. The prince of Wales, after years of waiting in the wings, was at last king. Like George IV before him, he had suffered from the years of suspense. As Edward VII, he was to face the troubles and trials of the early twentieth century. Some historians claim that the worries over the threat of war abroad and violence at home helped to kill him.

'Propaganda of the deed'

Edward VII was king at a time when the very existence of monarchy was under threat. Again the threat was one of revolution. But now the revolutionaries included many of the working class people of Europe. The poor, the hungry, and ill-paid now drew their inspiration from the teaching of the German philosopher Karl Marx, and became Communists. They worked for a general revolution around the world when the kings, landlords and factory owners would be swept away. Swift individual action was required to gain publicity for the cause of revolution and, perhaps, to provoke rebellion itself. The 'anarchists', each one normally acting alone, sought to bring change through the 'Propaganda of the Deed' – by assassination of the rich and powerful. What better propaganda could there be than to kill a

king? In 1881, Alexander II, Tsar of Russia was blown to pieces by revolutionaries. In 1898 the emperor of Austria-Hungary's wife, the empress Elizabeth, was shot to death. The next few years saw Tsar Nicholas II lose an uncle and four ministers. The ranks of the royalty of Europe were thinned. Kingship was a dangerous business!

In 1905, Russia suffered her first revolution. Waves of strikes and deadly bombing attacks swept through France. Could Britain remain unaffected?

Ulster will fight and Ulster will be right

Another challenge came from Ireland. Liberal party governments had been trying to give self-government to the Irish for years. Gladstone tried in 1886 and 1893. The Conservative party was pledged to keep Ireland as part of the empire at all costs. By 1913, a Home Rule Bill had been passed by the Liberals, and would become law in 1914. The threat of Home Rule had long worried the Protestants in the North of Ireland. They would be heavily outnumbered by Catholics in a united Ireland. They began to arm themselves to defy the Liberal government.

Above: Archduke Franz Ferdinand, heir to the Austro–Hungarian throne, who was assassinated in 1914. A number of killings of notable people in the late 1800s and early 1900s led to a very uneasy time for the European monarchy.

Right: Ulster Day, 28 September, 1912, Sir Edward Carson (in the middle) is shown on his way to sign a covenant pledging to resist Home Rule.

Protestant defiance

The Conservatives encouraged this defiance. 'Ulster will fight and Ulster will be right', Randolph Churchill, a leading Conservative politician, had once said. Again, in 1912, Bonar Law, a future Conservative prime minister, stated, 'I can imagine no height of resistance to which Ulster will go in which I will not support them.'

In 1914, even the British army defied the legal government of Great Britain over the Irish problem. The British garrison at the Curragh, in Dublin, warned that any government order to use force to enforce the Home Rule Act against the Ulster Protestants would be disobeyed.

The challenge to Parliament

The traditional partnership of king, Lords and Commons was soon under threat. Many groups outside the male, property-owning, political system felt excluded and let down by Parliament. Many British women despaired of peacefully persuading an all-male House of Commons to grant female suffrage the right to vote. Emmeline Pankhurst's 'Suffragette' movement was founded in 1903 to fight for this right, and became increasingly violent. Suffragettes smashed windows, chained themselves to railings, and, on one occasion, divested an astonished Cabinet minister of his trousers. In 1913, a protester, Emily Davison, met her death when she hurled herself under the king's horse at the Derby (see below).

had once used this power, and, in 1832, William IV had threatened to do so. Edward VII, the largest landowner in the country, naturally sympathized with the Conservatives. At first he rejected Asquith's suggestions. 'I should certainly decline', he said, 'as I would far sooner be unpopular than ridiculous'. But the Liberals bullied the king. Edward's son, George, the prince of Wales, thought, 'they have treated him very shabbily – one can see by his letters how worried he is'. The king eventually gave in and agreed to help Asquith. However, when Edward died it was left to George V to renew Edward's pledge.

Edward VII and the peers crisis

Edward VII died in the middle of a difficult political crisis. It seemed in 1910 that the House of Commons and the House of Lords had come to a deadlock. In 1906, a Liberal government had come to power with an enormous majority of seats in the House of Commons. The Liberals proceeded to bring in new laws to help the Trade Unions, the poor and the unemployed. But the Conservative party used its many friends in the House of Lords to block the Liberal laws. The Conservatives feared that the balance of power in British politics was swinging away from the land and property-owning classes whom they represented, and towards the working and poorer classes led by the Liberals. To use the power of the House of Lords to block the new laws was therefore an act of self-defence.

When the Lords rejected the Budget of 1909, the fight was on. Herbert Asquith, the Liberal prime minister remembered that the king had the power to create peers. If Edward created hundreds of Liberal peers, they could then out-vote the Conservatives. Queen Anne

Far left: Emily Davison's sacrifice for the cause of votes for women. She died the day after she had thrown herself under the king's horse at the Derby.

The threat to create peers was enough. The Lords gave in. From then on their power to block laws was reduced. They could only delay legislation for two years. The two kings, Edward VII and George V, had reluctantly, but conscientiously, cooperated to save the British political system. □

1 When a suffragette died at the Derby many people felt sorrier for the horse and rider! Do you think the suffragette was right?

2 Try to find out who the suffragists were. Was their aim helped by the suffragettes?

3 The House of Lords still exists. Its debates are shown regularly on television. Make a point of watching a debate. Draw a picture and describe what you see.

Above: The Peers Crisis of 1909–1911 resulted in a great reduction in the power of the House of Lords. King Edward VII died in the middle of the crisis. His successor, George V, acted fairly and kept the promise to create Liberal peers if necessary.

11 War and peace

Although threatened by anarchy and assassination, the monarchs of Europe seemed to be making the most of their last years of wealth and luxury before the outbreak of World War I in 1914. Queen Victoria's large family had spread throughout Europe.

European connections

Victoria's grandchildren included the empress of Russia, and kaiser of Germany. Other relatives forged links with the thrones of Spain, Norway, Romania, and Greece. To be a monarch was to be a member of a small, rich, private club. Even as war threatened, Kaiser Wilhelm and Tsar Nicholas wrote letters to 'Dear Willy' and 'Dear Nicky'.

Edward VII was especially at ease within this magic circle. He had spent years as a prince in constant travel, in search for amusement. When the British government needed friends in a hostile world, Edward was encouraged to use his travels to further his country's foreign policy. As a 'diplomat' king he created another important role for a modern monarchy.

Above right: King George V (seated centre) is surrounded by eight of the European monarchs who attended king Edward VII's funeral.

Above left: Nicky (Tsar Nicholas II) and George, prince of Wales (on the right) in 1909.

Below: The two 'armed camps' of Europe in 1900.

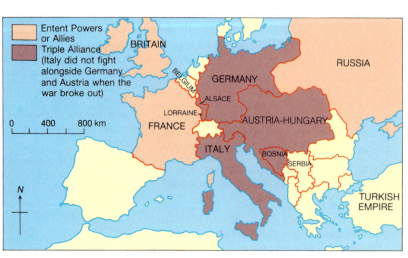

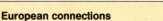

War clouds

By 1900, Europe was divided into two armed camps (see map). The main threat to peace seemed to be Germany. Germany was a new country. It had been united in 1871, after inflicting a humiliating defeat upon France. The French had never forgiven the Germans; the Germans could never feel safe from a French war of revenge. To remain secure, Germany relied on an alliance with her neighbour, Austria–Hungary. A worried France grasped the chance to ally with Russia. No amount of 'Willy-Nicky' letters could disguise the hostility between the two alliances. Only Britain was left out. Envied for her colonial possessions, Britain was friendless and isolated.

Worse, Britain relied upon her enormous navy to keep her shores and her empire safe. Yet, from 1899 onward, Kaiser Wilhelm's Germany challenged Britain by building a navy.

A king in Paris

Britain turned instead to France. Edward VII, the one-time playboy of Parisian night-life, was to smooth over plans for a new Anglo-French friendship. It was not to be easy. The king was booed on arrival in Paris in 1903. 'The French don't like us', he remarked, 'why should they?' But Edward's charm, his fluent French, and a

Map legend:
- Entent Powers or Allies
- Triple Alliance (Italy did not fight alongside Germany and Austria when the war broke out)

BRITAIN
RUSSIA
BELGIUM
GERMANY
ALSACE
LORRAINE
FRANCE
AUSTRIA-HUNGARY
ITALY
BOSNIA
SERBIA
TURKISH EMPIRE

0   400   800 km

N

fine speech at the magnificent official banquet won them over. Though they were Republicans, the French cheered, 'Vive notre roi' ('Long live *our* King'). In 1904 Edward's diplomacy helped seal an *entente cordiale*, a friendly agreement between the British and the French.

Thereafter the foreign office encouraged the king's overseas visits. Edward was sometimes unenthusiastic:

66 The foreign Office, to gain their own object will not care a pin what humiliation I have to put up with. 99

The war to end all wars

But Edward's best efforts turned out to be in vain. War broke out in 1914, four years after Edward's death. The problems of modern war and politics were a grim inheritance for the new king, George V.

George was an ex-naval officer who had not expected to become king. However, his elder brother, Albert, had died in 1892. A Liberal prime minister, Lord Rosebery, thought George's naval training was an advantage. He was pleased that George:

66 has expressed his interest in the Empire by memorable words and deeds ... He means to do for the Empire what king Edward did for the peace of Europe. 99

King George V and Queen Mary visited India in 1905, and, in 1911, they were actually crowned there.

Then, in July 1914, the assassination of archduke Franz Ferdinand (see page 22) sparked off the crisis which led to World War I. The war plans of the Germans and the Russians needed swift action, too swift for diplomats to resolve the crisis. When Germany invaded Belgium, the empire went to the defence of Belgium and France. George now found an important function as a national leader in wartime. He made countless visits to inspect troops, dockyards and hospitals, and he and his sons visited the front-line in France. One prince, Edward, actually fought at the naval Battle of Jutland in 1916.

Changing names

During the war, anything German came under attack. German shops in London were looted. People with German names were beaten up.

Above: The Great Durbar, Delhi, December 1911. When George V was armed Emperor of India.

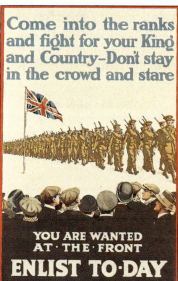

Left: A recruiting poster appealing to people's loyalty to their king.

Army and government officials, like prince Louis of Battenberg, and the war minister, lord Haldane, who had strong German connections were forced to resign. The royal family was embarrassed. Everyone knew that the ancestors of George V were German. And so, in July 1917, the royal family's old German name of Saxe-Coburg was dropped. The royal family took the name of Windsor instead. A German writer sadly commented, 'the royal tradition died when, for a mere war, George V changed his name.' □

1 Why was it difficult to become friends with the French? How do we get on with France and Germany in the present day?

2 The monarchs of Europe are worried and want peace. Hold an emergency debate between Nicky, Willy, George, and Franz Josef (Emperor of Austria). Why do you think kings and emperors were *unable* to stop the war in 1914?

"There seems to be a regular epidemic of revolutions and abdications throughout the enemy countries which certainly makes it a hard and critical time for the remaining monarchies.**"** (Albert, Prince of Wales, later King Edward VIII)

In 1918, a young prince Albert was right to worry. At the end of World War I, the defeated nations turned on their rulers. Kaiser Wilhelm of Germany slunk into exile while armed bands of communists and demoralized soldiers fought out a revolution on the streets of Germany. The Hapsburg empire of Austria-Hungary had disappeared. Such revolutions might spread to the countries of the victors including Britain:

Russian revolution

Meanwhile, an entire royal family, that of Tsar Nicholas of Russia, fell victim to the Bolsheviks, the communist founders of the present-day Soviet Union. The Bolsheviks then appealed for revolution throughout the world.

Тов. Ленин ОЧИЩАЕТ землю от нечисти.

Right: The Bolsheviks fought for control of society by the workers. This Russian cartoon shows Lenin ridding the world of the wealthy people.

'What would grandmama have thought?'

King George V took a relaxed view.

"I went to a football match at which there were 73,000 people: at the end they sang the National Anthem. There were no Bolsheviks there! The Country is all right.**"**

British Socialists of the Labour Party were rather moderate compared to the Bolsheviks. Even so, when George summoned the first Labour government to office in 1924, he did wonder what his 'Grandmama', Victoria, would have thought of such a government. Could socialists and a monarchy mix?

George and his two sons, who followed him as kings, were realists. In the face of problems like poverty and unemployment, George himself explained to the government after World War I, that:

"it is impossible to expect people to live upon the unemployment benefit. The King appeals to the Government to meet this grave difficulty as generously as they did in dealing with the enormous daily cost of the war.**"**

If the British chose a socialist Labour government, then, in George's words, 'True to British ideas, the Government, whoever they should be, should have a fair chance'.

His master's voice

The early twentieth century was a period full of new inventions which changed everyone's lives. The monarchy, naturally, was affected by the motor car, the telegraph and the radio. Queen Victoria's jubilee of 1897 provided a sign of change. The queen empress was delighted to send her jubilee message around the world by telegraph. Her son, Edward VII, used the new technology too. He was an early, though reckless, motorist.

During the hard times of the 1930s, George V pioneered an important new technique, which has since become a tradition – the royal broadcast. He also started the idea of the annual Christmas message. The first of these was broadcast in 1932 and became a regular feature of George's reign. George V became steadily more popular with the British public. The monarch was no longer a distant figure, but a familiar voice in the home.

George's son, Edward VIII, was an enthusiastically 'modern' figure. He used radio broadcasts and made a point of making his first journey as king by aeroplane. Edward's brother, George VI, was shyer and more old-fashioned. However, the demands of wartime (World War II, 1939–45) forced him to use the radio. When war broke out in September 1939, King George VI spoke to his people, 'in this grave hour, as if I were able to cross your threshold and speak to you myself.' The monarchy was firmly part of the twentieth century.

All for love

In December 1936, King Edward VIII, who had only become king in January, gave up the throne to his younger brother, George VI. Edward, a popular, handsome war-hero, had fallen for a married woman. His chosen wife was an American called Mrs Simpson. She was twice married – and still married! Edward wanted to marry her *and* keep the throne. In his own words:

66 All my life I trained for the job. For a year as King I worked as hard and selflessly as I knew how. Of course I wished to be King. More, I wished to remain King. 99

The prime minister, Stanley Baldwin, was unimpressed. He thought Edward had, 'the mind of a child' and 'was absolutely devoid of any appreciation of his responsibilities.' The royal family, too, rallied round Queen Mary, the queen mother, and insisted that Edward could *either* remain king *or* marry Mrs Simpson. He could not do both. The king chose to abdicate. He broadcast his decision to the nation and went abroad, taking the title of duke of Windsor.

George VI, reacted to his sudden promotion with something resembling panic. To his friend, Lord Mountbatten, he confessed:

66 This is terrible – I never wanted this to happen. I'm quite unprepared for it. I'm only a naval officer. It's the only thing I know about. 99

Another major crisis was over, but the years of peace were coming to an end. For George the ordeal of modern war was soon to begin. □

Left: King George V was the first British king to use the radio to reach his people. He started the tradition of the Christmas broadcast in 1932. The news of his death in 1936 reached every part of the empire within seconds.

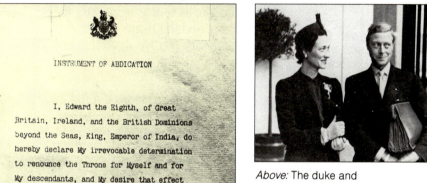

Above: The duke and duchess of Windsor.

Left: The document by which king Edward VIII gave up the throne.

1 The winners of World War 1, France, America and Great Britain, did not suffer from revolution. They were all democracies. Do you think democracy helped them: a) avoid revolution; b) win the war?

2 Labour politicians weren't used to royalty. They even had to hire suits to wear to see the king! As a Labour minister, describe your hopes and fears for your first meeting with George V. Do you think the Labour ministers should have dressed up specially to meet the king? Would you?

3 Do you think Edward VIII made the right choice? Do you think the British should have let him marry Mrs Simpson *and* remain king?

George VI was fated to be king during World War II. He and his wife, Queen Elizabeth (later a much-loved queen mother), threw themselves into their work. When, in 1940, Buckingham Palace was bombed by the Germans, the queen said:

> **"**I'm glad we've been bombed – it makes me feel I can look the East End in the face. **"**

And they did tour the badly bombed East End of London, as well as inspecting the fire services, troops and the Home Guard. A visit to Coventry, a city terribly devastated by air raids in autumn 1940, was especially appreciated. A victim commented:

> **"**We suddenly felt that if the King was there, everything was alright and the rest of England was behind us. **"**

Below: The royal family and Winston Churchill on the balcony at Buckingham Palace on VE (Victory in Europe) Day. The war-time precaution of boarding up the windows is still in evidence.

The tradition, dating back to Victoria's visits to her injured soldiers (see page 21), lived on.

But George's patriotism was further tested at the end of the war. The damage and cost of the war effort helped to weaken Britain's grip on the empire. Soon the union jack was to be hauled down all over the world. First to go was India, in 1947, followed by Burma in 1948, and Palestine in 1948. Africans and Asians alike clamoured for independence. The Labour government, which came to power in 1945, was happy to oblige. George VI was the last king-emperor.

Indian Independence

The Indian demand for independence, led by Jawarharlal Nehru and Mahatma Gandhi, seemed irresistable. Yet, independence was a touchy and difficult process. Hindus would live in India, but Muslims wanted to break away and form a new state, Pakistan. The job of freeing India and setting up Pakistan went to a member of the royal family. George's close friend, lord Louis Mountbatten was 'the one man', thought the king, 'who might pull it off'. Mountbatten became the last viceroy (governor) of India. Despite violence and intrigue between Muslim and Hindu, he succeeded. In 1947 the independent states of India and Pakistan came into being.

Louis Mountbatten, Viceroy of India.

Changing times

After 1945, the monarchy had to adjust to the world of the atom bomb, and the jet aircraft. Britain was slow to recover from the war. Hard times and food rationing went on for years. The new prime minister, Clement Attlee thought the king, 'rather the worrying type'. George VI was worn out. He died in 1952 and the crown passed to his daughter, Queen Elizabeth II.

The new Elizabethans

Elizabeth's coronation was the first spectacular television event of the British monarchy. Much was made of her name, which reminded people of the great Tudor queen of the sixteenth century, Elizabeth I. Newspapers prophesied a 'New Elizabethan Age'. Prosperity returned in the 1950s. Jobs were plentiful, wages rose, and a Conservative prime minister, Harold Macmillan, told the British 'you've never had it so good'.

The Commonwealth

66 The Crown is a human link between all peoples who owe allegiance to me – an allegiance of mutual love and respect and never of compulsion. 99

(*Queen Elizabeth II*,
talking about the Commonwealth)

Britain's empire changed into a loose association known as the Commonweath. The new countries now ran their own affairs, but most remained within this voluntary organization. They recognized the queen as the 'human link', between the countries of an old empire. A tradition, expressed in Queen Victoria's jubilee telegraph of 1897, continues in Queen Elizabeth's involvement in regular commonwealth conferences. Frequent royal visits to commonwealth countries, and special mention of the 'Third World' in Christmas messages helped to preserve the Commonwealth relationship.

Batting for Britain

Once, when questioned about official visits abroad, the Conservative prime minister, Margaret Thatcher, explained she thought of herself as 'Batting for Britain' – that is fighting for British interests. Queen Elizabeth II has frequently found herself fulfilling the same function. Like Edward VII, she has become used to foreign office advice. This can cause problems. In 1980, for instance, a visit to Morocco went badly wrong. The queen and her husband, Prince Philip, were kept waiting for hours on end, missed meals, and were fobbed off with meetings with minor Moroccan princes. Photographs of the queen's eventual meeting with King Hassan V showed her glaring politely but freezingly at the offending monarch. A

spokesman commented, 'the queen has never been so angry'. But the trip had to go on despite this. British business contracts in Morocco were at stake.

The interests of the superpowers can also override and embarrass the British monarchy's official position. In autumn 1983, for instance, the island of Grenada, of which Elizabeth II was queen, was invaded by marines from the USA. The Americans claimed that Governor-General Paul Scoon had requested their help against the Marxist government of Grenada. All the signs were that the British government, and the queen, had been unaware of any such request.

Above: Queen Elizabeth II on the occasion of her coronation on June 2 1952.

Below: The queen shows her displeasure at being kept waiting during a royal visit to Morocco in 1980.

29

In other cases, royal diplomacy does still have some useful influence. Many Commonwealth leaders maintained power for decades after independence. Figures like Kenneth Kaunda of Zambia, and Hastings Banda of Malawi, and many other presidents and prime ministers in Africa and Asia frequently confer with the queen. As a result, for instance, a fraught and difficult process such as the ending of civil war in Southern Rhodesia (now Zimbabwe) in 1980, could be smoothed over.

Below: A modern cartoon that mocks royalty. Compare this with the cartoon of the royal family on page 13.

"...nockout idea for our next James Bond movie!"

Above: A caricature of members of the royal family by the 'Spitting Image' team.

Right: By tradition, the queen opens Parliament by reading a speech declaring the plans of the government for the year.

"All the things My Government is going to do in 1987"

Royal powers

Royal powers showed themselves to be alive and well in 1975 in Australia, and again, in 1982 in Canada. In Australia, a left-wing prime minister found himself dismissed by the queen's representative, governor-general Sir John Kerr. Kerr used the royal power of dismissal and appointment against prime minister Gough Whitlam, during a political crisis. Needless to say, this move was not at all popular with all Australians, many of whom called for a republic.

> **Royal prestige**
> In Canada, the queen was called upon to help prime minister Pierre Trudeau pass a new constitution for his country. No doubt, Trudeau could have managed without help, but royal prestige strengthened his hand against opponents of the deal.

So the queen retains some important power and influence at home and abroad. In Britain, she can declare or end wars, dismiss, summon or suspend Parliament, and veto its laws. She is 'the sole fount of honour'. This means, in practice, that she puts her name to the New Year, and birthday honours list. Twice a year, sportsmen, entertainers, politicians and civil servants are awarded the Order of the British Empire (OBE), knighthoods or other honours. In reality, the honours are a way for the prime minister to reward successful or loyal subjects with a knighthood or a medal.

The power to dissolve Parliament, and, consequently, to call for a general election can still have great significance. In 1957 and 1963, when Conservative prime ministers resigned from office, and in 1974, when Harold Wilson (Labour) only narrowly won an election, the queen's own political decisions were vital. She took the advice of Conservative politicians in choosing the new prime ministers in 1957 and 1963. In 1974, she chose to grant Mr Wilson a second chance to appeal to the voters in a general election.

A good thing?

66 This I do believe, is the system mankind has so far evolved – to which, rightly or wrongly I belong and which I represent to the best of my ability – is one of the strongest factors in the continuance of stable government. 99

(*Prince Charles*, 1974)

By the late 1970s and early 1980s, the British monarchy was perhaps more popular than at any time in its existence. Scenes of wild enthusiasm greeted such royal events as the queen's jubilee in 1977, the weddings of the prince and princess of Wales in 1981 and of the duke and duchess of York in 1986, and the birth of Elizabeth's grandchildren. Press and television coverage became almost hysterical at times, and was rarely critical of the monarchy. Clearly, the monarchy is seen as a 'good thing' by a large section of the British public. Yet it is an expensive institution, costing tax-papers many thousands of pounds. It must be noted that the *empty* palaces of long-gone foreign kings generate similar tourist interest abroad.

It is a long time since there has been a genuine republican movement in Britain. We have seen the British royal family adapt to changing times and to bring in new blood from abroad when necessary. A popular and effective role has been built up, notably by George III, Victoria and by the 'New Elizabethans' in taking the lead in morality and as the head of society. Yet the dangers of life without monarchy have receded. The dreaded chaos of Cromwell's time (see page 6), or of the French or Russian revolutions (see pages 12 and 26) are hardly a threat in a world full of successful republics such as France and the USA. We cannot dispute the British monarchy's contribution to the history of stable government in Britain. We cannot deny its success and popularity in the late twentieth century. But we can ask ourselves: is it now a luxury, or a necessity? □

1 George V was sad to lose India. What sort of message do you think he would have sent to its new rulers?

2 You may well have seen the queen's Christmas broadcasts. What sort of scenes do the broadcasts show of: a) her family; b) the Commonwealth?

3 Do you think after reading this book that the monarchy is good, or bad. Hold a class discussion and take a vote.

4 Look at the various cartoons. Now try some yourself. Draw a cartoon of the queen, prince Philip, prince Andrew, prince Charles and princess Diana.

5 Read and cut out anything you can find in papers and magazines about the royal family. Do you think the monarchy is still popular with most people?

Above: This street party was held to celebrate queen Elizabeth II's Silver Jubilee. There were also many official ceremonies and services (look back to page 20 for queen Victoria's celebrations).

Left: Prince Charles, the heir to the throne, with his family. Are they just the ordinary people we see here, or are they really something special?

31

Index

Illustration references are shown in heavy type

Acknowledgements

The publishers would like to thank the following for permission to reproduce photographs:

AA Picture Library, pp. 14 (bottom), 18 top; Associated Press, p. 28 (right); BBC Hulton Picture Library, pp. 16, 22 (bottom), 25 (top), 27 (bottom and right); Bridgeman Art Library, p. 8 (top); British Museum, p. 11; Camera Press, p. 24 (right); Central Independent TV, p. 30 (bottom left); Daily Mirror, p. 30 (top and bottom); Edimedia, pp. 12, 26; Fotomas, p. 15 (bottom); John Freeman, pp. 10 (top), 15 (bottom); Illustrated London News, p. 21 (right); Imperial War Museum, pp. 21 (left), 25 (bottom); Keystone Collection, pp. 28 (left), 29 (top); Mansell Collection, pp. 13 (top), 14 (top); National Army Museum, p. 21 (top); National Library of Ireland, p. 15 (top); National Portrait Gallery, pp. 7, 8 (bottom), 13 (bottom); Robert Opie Collection, p. 19 (bottom); Popperfoto pp. 22 (top), 23, 27 (top); Punch pp. 17 (bottom), 19 (top); Rex Features, pp. 4, 29 (bottom), 31 (both); Royal Collection (Reproduced by Gracious Permission of Her Majesty the Queen), pp. 6, 7 (right), 9 (top), 10 (bottom), 16 (top), 18 (bottom), 20, 24 (left); Tate Gallery, p. 9 (bottom); V & A, p. 17 (top)

Illustrations by John Ireland

Cover illustration: Queen Victoria in her coronation robes, 1837, (Royal Collection, reproduced by Gracious Permission of Her Majesty the Queen)

Oxford University Press, Walton St, Oxford OX2 6DP

Oxford New York Toronto
Delhi Bombay Calcutta Madras Karachi
Petaling Jaya Singapore Hong Kong Tokyo
Nairobi Dar es Salaam Cape Town
Melbourne Auckland

and associated companies in

Berlin Ibadan
Oxford is a trademark of Oxford University Press

© **Oxford University Press 1989**

ISBN 0 19 913318 2 (limp, non-net)
ISBN 0 19 913349 2 (cased, net)

Typesetting by MS Filmsetting Limited, Frome, Somerset
Printed in Hong Kong